Dedication

This book is dedicated to all those committed to making a difference while they are here. In the end, we are only caretakers of our material possessions. We can't take anything with us. Therefore, the only thing that really matters is "it mattered that we were here." – Kevin McNeely

Foreword

My third book "Diary of an Everyday Millionaire: My Secrets to Building a Real Estate Empire" was filled with general knowledge. I feel like it was a good book when it was written but times have changed now. I've changed. Over the years, my thinking as an investor has matured. I'm doing some things differently now. In our world, the only constant is change and I need to change with the world in order to stay competitive and survive. Since "Diary of an Everyday Millionaire", I have gained more education, knowledge and experience with the various financial instruments so my tactics, technique and procedures have naturally shifted, changed and developed as a result.

A few of readers asked for more meat and potatoes in my books. They asked for more specifics. I've heard their feedback and I have responded. In this book, I give anyone who reads it, a deeper dive into my mind and more specifics into why I do the things that I do.

I discuss my thoughts, experiences and strategies in greater detail. I even discuss some of the specific tools I use to find real estate deals and manage my ever-growing portfolio of properties. Ultimately, readers get a chance to see what makes me tick. I'm a complex individual with complex thoughts. I strive to think outside the box and do things differently from the masses.

In a Q&A session, I answer specific questions. It is a no-holds-barred session. I give up quality nuggets of data, including specifics on numbers and tips on property management and cost cutting. It is the most valuable part of this book in my opinion and I'm confident even seasoned investors will get something out of it.

I will tell everyone upfront, there is no fast way to make money. There is no risk-free path to wealth either. The road to wealth is tough and littered with setbacks and obstacles. If anyone is looking for fast money, this book won't help. This book is about me and my experiences as an investor. I'm certain readers will find the information within its pages useful but if they don't, I fully encourage them to return it for a refund.

Since the birth of land rights, real estate has made more fortunes than any other investment vehicle. Real estate is the foundation of all things. Its value is, and always will be timeless. Humans have and always will, depend on real estate for survival. That is why real estate is so important to us.

However, owning income properties is more than just wealth accumulation. There is a social responsibility too. When real estate is cared for and properly managed, it provides someone with a home. It provides lifesaving shelter and it is a place where new generations of Americans grow and live. Real estate is a key part in a person's quality of life. Investors can make a real difference in the world with real estate. It is more than just a commodity. It is a place where lives happen. That is why I really wrote this book. I want all investors to know my true feelings about property. It is my hope that my way of thinking changes others. I hope I never hear the words "it's just a rental" again because it isn't, their rental is someone's home. Property owners are entrusted with something magical. The quality of life of hardworking people are tied to their properties. It is a great responsibility and it is time property owners view it as such. They need to wake everyday with the idea…today, I will make a difference first, profits come second.

Introduction

I'm a normal guy. I live in an average middle class neighborhood in Texas. Every morning I open the garage and sip coffee while I enjoy the quietness of the neighborhood. I watch kids load school buses and I watch parents begin their daily commute to work. Technically, I'm unemployed. I'm a statistic. I have no job.

The reality is I'm retired. I'm 45 years old. I've been retired for a few years now. Money isn't an issue for me. I find it more of a challenge to fill my time. Retirement wasn't what I imagined especially since I was a hard-charging individual used to a very hectic life. Retirement turned out to be depressing. The days were too slow for me so I started writing this book and others as a diversion to fill my time.

Although I know there are some good nuggets of information in this book, this isn't a "how to" book. This isn't advice of any kind either. I don't recommend anything I do. Truthfully, I don't care if anyone ever reads this book. It is more of a deep dive into my millionaire mind. I started writing it for fun but it changed into an exploration into how I got where I am today. I wanted to understand myself and how I think. Ultimately, this book exists for my personal enjoyment but if others want to take a look into my mind, I applaud them. There are some good things in there however, I warn readers to keep their expectations low and don't expect much. A real estate license will likely reap them more benefits than reading this book. Now having said that, if I choose to publish this book, I'm certain readers will learn many things from it. It is filled with my personal thoughts and experiences. It's almost as if I'm at a psychiatrist, laying on a sofa, downloading my financial thoughts and opinions. I'm expecting a short book, maybe about 50 pages or so and I don't think it'll take me very long to write it. I'm guessing a few days. Once I start writing, it's hard for me to stop. Most of my other books were written in just days too. As I'm writing, I'll bold key words and phrases. I'm doing this largely for me. As I said, I want to understand myself and I want to understand why I do the things I do. If I publish this book, I'm certain I won't sell it for much.

It's a book written without plan or system. I don't even have an outline. I'm just writing. I'm 100% certain I won't market it. I will just throw it out there and a lucky few will come across it. I feel a few bucks is appropriate compensation for my thoughts and opinions. It is kind of like inviting me out for coffee or lunch.

Inside My Millionaire Mind

Memoirs of a Millionaire Investor

Kevin McNeely, MBA

This publication is designed to provide accurate and authoritative information in regard to the subject matter covered. It is sold with the understanding that the publisher or author is not engaged in rendering legal, accounting, or other professional service. If legal advice or other expert assistance is required, the services of a competent professional person should be sought.

Editor: Kevin McNeely
Cover Design: Kevin McNeely
Typesetting: Kevin McNeely

© 2018 by Kevin McNeely
Self published by Kevin McNeely
All rights reserved. The text of this publication, or any part thereof, may not be reproduced in any manner whatsoever without the written permission from the publisher or author.
Printed in the United States of AmericaVersion 1.0

Copyright © 2018 Kevin McNeely

All rights reserved.

This work is licensed under Kevin McNeely

You buy my coffee and I share my financial story with you. In my mind, this isn't a book. I guess it is more of a conversation between two friends. Just imagine, we are sitting in a local coffee shop. You just brought me a coffee and you asked 'How did you get where you are today?" And I start talking…

Chapter 1

When I first retired. I struggled with the concept. I struggled to fill my time. I had a sizable stock account but it didn't requirement much management. I had two rental properties with a local property manager and I had tons and tons of time. To this day, I'm not sure how it fully happened but life pulled me in the direction of real estate. I suppose it all happened by luck, circumstance and chance. I think a lot of people have no idea what they want to be when they grow up and life pulls people in certain directions. Life pulled me towards real estate.

When I first started to get serious about real estate investing. I focused on the acquisition of new assets. I'd buy properties, renovate them and turn them over to a local property management company. Over time a span of three years, I experienced rapid growth. I increased my real estate holdings from three properties to 14 properties. Twelve of the those are currently rentals.

The properties gross about $10,000 a month. Once the debt is serviced and expenses are taken out, I clear over $3,200 monthly. It may not seem like much but for Texas, it goes a long way. I don't know, call me simple minded but $3,200 a month seems like a lot to earn for just sleeping. My stock accounts add an additional $1,000 a month to my coffers and I have a decent government pension too. With all my sources of income, I earn about $8,300 a month sleeping. Since I have a humble lifestyle; I never spend all of my earning either. Don't get me wrong, I travel often and have loads fun. My kids are I are always taking a road trip. Yearly, we take an out of state vacation. We experience restaurants on the regular. We spend but we spend wisely.

Despite the black card in my wallet, we still use Groupon. We shop for school clothes at Burlington and Ross. I skip the expensive retail stores and buy my suits for $200 max. I shop for bargain vacation packages and I still use coupons. The way I view it is every dollar I save is a dollar I can spend on more fun. Because of the way I have designed my life, I find it difficult to spend all I earn. Every month I have thousands left over. I use any surplus money to either invest or pay down real estate debt. Whichever gives me the greatest return at the moment. Every month I find my expenses decrease and/or my profits increase. Every month I get wealthier. How did I get here?

It is a long story. You'll find some of my story chronicled in my previous books: "Get Rich Off A Minimum Wage Income" and "Diary of an Everyday Millionaire:

My Secrets to Building a Real Estate Empire." I wrote those books years ago. Over time, my strategies towards wealth accumulation have changed and morphed with the times. I used to think buying a home wasn't a good idea. Now I think it's essential to building wealth. I used to think buying older rentals wasn't the best idea. Now I think older rentals cash flow a lot better and investment dollars in underserved neighborhoods benefit everyone. If an older home is renovated, it can increase its market value. This increases the market value of every home on the block. This increases taxation for the county which allows more spending on essential goods and services like schools and police. Quality schools bring in higher income earning residents and police presence increases security. Security brings in business investment and jobs and the cycle of positive change for a neighborhood continues until it peaks. As I'm writing this book. I have no format. No outline. It's just me and a computer downloading my thoughts. Nothing in this book is meant to be advice for anyone. I don't plan on actually marketing it at all. I just have this inner need to just write today. It's been years since I wrote a book and if anyone would have ever asked me if I'd write another, my answer would have been "no." Maybe it's the coffee surging through my veins or maybe it's just an inner need to write but I have an urge to write today.

So how did I get here today? Well, for starters I had the right mindset from the beginning. I grew up really poor and I always wanted to be wealthy. I didn't want it for fancy clothes or fast cars. I just wanted it for the security money brings. It's good to know if you need to go to the dentist, you can. It's good to know that if you need food, you can go buy some. It's just good to know your needs are met. It gives you a feeling of safety and security. The first thing I did to get me where I am today is I picked the right career. I chose to pursue a career in the military.

I joined the military in 1992 and I served 23 years. It was a very turbulent two decades. Since 2001, the United States has been in continuous conflict. I physically deployed to two wars and a peace-keeping operation. I've been under constant mortar fire. Overall, I like to think I earned that retirement. It is important to note, in the military, I met my first investor. In the mid-1990s, I met a military officer who was a passionate believer in mutual funds. Before I met him, I hadn't even heard of mutual funds. I didn't know what a mutual fund was.

For whatever reason, this officer took an interest in me. He passionately explained every detail about mutual funds to me. He explained what they were and how these financial instruments worked. I soaked up the information like a sponge. I quickly sought out more information. I read book after book. After building a decent knowledge base in the subject; I dived in and I started investing in funds.

This is where I got my start. Having the knowledge, I have today. I feel like mutual funds alone never got me wealthy. These instruments are designed to minimize risk. They are so diversified; the risk is taken down to a bare minimum. The SEC regulates funds heavily in an effort to protect citizens from loss. The risk is minimized through diversification. However, when risk is minimized, reward is stifled too.

Throughout the late 1990s, I continued to read everything I could get my hands on about investing. Eventually, I ran into a young man who earned less income than me but had a much larger bank account. He invested in individual stocks. I immediately became very interested in this financial instrument. I did what I knew best. I read books. After a couple of years of reading, I started buying individual stocks. With individual stocks, the risk is great but potential reward is great too. I learned quickly through loss that stocks aren't passive investments. I learned these financial instruments require significant study and due diligence. Over time, through trial and error, I learned to master these financial instruments too.

Stocks ruled my investment portfolio for years. After doing some reading, in 2011, I brought my first rental property. I still own that property today. My first exploration into rental property wasn't a success. I was inexperienced in negotiation so I overpaid for the property. It was an older house so it needed repairs. I had to replace the roof within a year. I didn't have any knowledge or experience of routine expenses associated with rental property.

Income property expenses are considerable. There are mortgage payments, repairs, taxes, insurance, legal and maintenance fees. The cost can quickly add up and chew up most of the monthly rent. Don't get me wrong, I love real estate as an investment but it wasn't a sure thing like real estate brokers or gurus wanted me to believe. Over time, I learned real estate brokers make their living off commissions and gurus make their wealth off of selling courses so they want everyone to believe in real estate. No doubt, real estate is a powerful investment but not all the time. It has to be purchased at the right price and under the right market conditions. I found out this key lesson as I gained experience.

From 2011 to present, I've spent my time accumulating rentals. I've gone from three properties in 2015 to 14 now. That's an addition of 11 properties in four years. I could have had more. However, as I've gained experience, I've become a more disciplined investor. I think the greatest lesson I've learned over my decades of investing in various assets is discipline. **I've learned to wait and purchase**

investments at the right price and time. There is no greater lesson than that. Whatever the investment is, I learned to purchase it under market value.

I'm no crook or vulture either. I don't cheat anyone. I'm actually performing a vital service for others. I'm helping people get out of a bad situation. I help them raise money fast so they can meet their obligations. People may need to sell a property for a variety of reasons. Most of the time, they have overextended themselves and taken on too much debt and they need to raise cash fast. It's hard to believe but people put themselves in some tough situation using borrowed money. When their debt burden become too large, they start selling assets and that's when I start buying.

It's been a long journey for me to get to this point. It was once a difficult thing to standby and not invest when the stock market reached a new high every day. I felt like I was missing out on something. There were times when I felt like the market was going to go up forever. Buying during those times have always resulted in great financial loss for me. On the flip side, it's not easy buying any asset in a down market. News agency talk about doom and gloom every day for ratings. People love drama and media companies give them what they want. It's difficult to ignore the noise and buy during these times. I remember thinking the stock market was going to collapse to zero in 2008. The best investors brought during those times and I argue one of the best investments were banks. After the Lehman Brothers bankruptcy, the government told everyone in advance that it would bail the remaining banks out. The government said the banks were simply too big to fail. For those with the courage to go for it, banks were probably the easiest and most financially rewarding investment of our time.

I missed it. I personally didn't have the courage to go for it. I was a big mistake. I don't cry over spilled milk or missed opportunities because I know modern economies are fueled by emotion rather than critical thought and due diligence. Another bust is coming. And financial busts open the door to opportunities for the prepared. In fact, throughout history, human economies go through a continual cycle of boom and bust. It's extremely hard to see them coming but there are signs. **I monitor consumer debt and asset prices to attempt to predict busts.** I say "attempt" because predicting anything is just plain hard.

Why do I watch consumer debt level? Investors borrow money to buy things. Maybe it's stocks, rental property or even a business. The more they borrow; the higher prices rise. At some point, the income their investments generate can't keep up with their debt payments and the bubble pops. If this happens to several investors at the same time, investors rush to sell assets. With everyone selling assets at the same time, the market is flooded and assets prices fall. This starts an economic bust cycle. When assets prices fall to low levels, they become attractive to credit worthy investors like me and I start buying again. The cycle begins again with a new boom. This boom and bust cycle has been going on since the beginning of time and I've attempted to profit from it. For the most part, I have. It's the middle of 2018 right now. The stock market is at new highs, property values are up and consumer debt is higher than it was in 2008. I've made a conscious choice to stack cash at this point. I feel like a bust is coming soon but truthfully, it's anybody's guess. Honestly, I just can't find any good investments out there right now. Everything is expensive. I look at the price of assets relative to the income they produce. Right now, nothing really looks good. I haven't seen anything I'd consider a home run for a long time. Getting back to my chronicles of how I arrived at this point, stocks really have been a vehicle to get me here. I'll talk a little more about stocks in the next chapter.

Chapter 2

have a simple strategy. **I like to invest in stocks that technology will never, ever replace. I'm really fond of food stocks.** I like stocks like Kraft Heinz. Nothing will ever replace a human's need for food. These are stocks I can hold forever without worry or stress. We may perfect self-driving cars one day and it may change the way we travel and our way of life but we'll still need to eat. No new technological advancement will ever change that fact. If humans still exist a million years from now; they will still need to eat. Nothing will ever change our need for nourishment. Because of that fact, food stocks are a solid investment to me. Whether it's a corporation producing eggs in Mexico or beef raised in good, ole America. Packaged food is the one industry I don't lose any sleep over. **Another industry I like is restaurants.** Although, restaurants are cyclical by nature, restaurants as an industry won't ever go away. Since ancient times, there have been restaurants in some form. **Basic materials matter to me.** Why? Basic materials are the foundation for all products. You cannot refine gas without oil. There isn't any plastic without oil. Whether it's copper, silver, lead, zinc or uranium; these elements are the key building blocks of many of the products that make up our way of life. It's possible we may invent something better than a cell phone one day but we'll need basic materials to create it. Now having said all that, I think valuation relative to earnings is most important.

The historical average price vs earning of the stock market is 15. **As a rule of thumb, I don't purchase stocks with a P/E over 15.** I actually prefer to buy stocks with a P/E under 10. I make it a point to buy undervalued securities. As a result, I don't find many stocks to buy. I may buy a couple of stocks a year but not many. I pick my own stocks too. Stock brokers and fund managers have tried to convince me they are more skilled at picking investments than me. I haven't seen any evidence of this. I'll be impressed when I meet a financial manager with a larger net worth than me. To date, I haven't met any so I remain unimpressed with the whole lot. **As a rule of thumb, a stock needs pays a dividend.** I prefer to buy stocks with a dividend yield greater than the current 10-year treasury yield. I rarely invest in anything that doesn't produce income. I don't see the point really. I feel a lifetime is short and I need income now. I rarely take a chance on speculative investments.

A speculative investment is an investment that you buy and hope someone later will pay you more for it. While you wait, it does nothing for you. It doesn't produce any income. Your only chance for profits is through stock appreciation.

In the meantime, the stock just sits there and looks pretty. For the most part, speculative investments are not my kind of investments. **The one exception I have for this rule depends on how big I think something could grow.** Uber is a good example.

In my opinion, Uber has a chance to reshape modern society with ridesharing. It can disrupt our whole way of life. I think if Uber ever goes public, I'll buy some shares because I think it can get really big. P/E and dividends don't matter to me if I believe some technology is revolutionary.

As a rule of thumb, I only invest in profitable companies. The best companies are profitable from the beginning. It shows good management is in place. It blows my mind why anyone would invest in a company not making a profit. Income and valuation are just part of the story when picking individual stocks. Strong brands matter.

Branding, when done correctly, can change our way of life. Coca-Cola is a fantastic example of powerful branding. In some parts of the country, all soda is referred to as Coke. I still find that such a curious thing. I remember ordering a soda in Oklahoma and the server asked me "What flavor of Coke do you want?" I told her orange. Like it or not, a strong brand becomes part of our American culture. It makes sense to pursue investing in these brands because it will take an incredible shift in our culture to make them obsolete. **Good numbers alone aren't enough to make me purchase a stock. There has to be a good story associated with the corporation.** What do I mean by a good story?

There has to be something happening to increase revenue in the future. At the time of this writing AT&T is looking to buy Time Warner. If this acquisition is permitted to proceed by the government, it'll likely increase revenues for the parent company. Here's another example. Apple recently brought Beats for $1 billion. The move expanded their product line and positioned the corporation to compete in the headset marketplace. The move permitted synergy between to iPhone and Beats branded cell phone accessories. This is what I mean by a good news story. Before I purchase any stock, I pour through its history of press releases and news articles looking for a good news story I can get behind. Whether is cost cutting, acquisitions, new products or share buy backs, I'm looking for some news…some nuggets…that will lead towards increasing earnings per share in the future. I try to find these good news stories before the overall market realizes what's going on. Now, there are plenty of stocks I avoid too.

Over the years, I've learned painful lessons by losing money. I steer clear of most technology stocks. **I rarely buy a technology stock but when I do, I don't risk much money.** Technology is loaded with risk. There is the possibility of fast riches and the possibility of rapid losses. Whenever I've purchased tech stocks, I've seen more losses than gains. Maybe it's my skills at tech stock analysis, maybe it's bad timing or just rotten luck. Whatever the reason, I know my limitations and I steer clear of technology stocks for the most part. We cannot live on stocks alone. We need other investments to compliment our portfolios and help weather a down stock market. That's why I buy corporate bonds too.

Corporate bonds are debt instruments. When I buy a bond, I'm simply loaning money to a corporation. The corporation promises to pay me back the principal plus interest. It's not much different from loaning money to a friend. Your friend defaults if they don't pay you back. Corporate bonds can default too.

The default rates of corporate bonds are relatively low. It's probably less under 2% over a 32-year period. However, the yields can be high. I personally invest in B rated bonds. These bonds are typically referred to "junk bonds." The risk is higher but if chosen correctly, so is the reward. At the time of this writing, there are many high yield bonds paying over 9%. At the time of this writing, in my saving account, I currently earn .09%. That's a massive different. That's why over the decades, I haven't saved much. I have over $1.4M in assets and I have less than $5,000 in savings. I learned very earlier on saving will not get you wealthy. Saving will not even get you financially secure. My thoughts are savings accounts benefit banks. I don't see any benefit for me. I recognize, saving accounts carry a lot less risk since my money is insured by the federal government. However, I stopped being risk adverse years ago so the fear of loss doesn't concern me. Now I embrace risk in all its form and I make calculated decisions to reduce it.

How do I pick corporate bonds? That's a good question. **My focus is on high yield bonds. I pour over a corporation's financials looking for current debt payments, assets and liabilities and cash flow.** It took me a lot of time and experience to get really good at it. <u>**The one steadfast rule of thumb I use is a corporation's debt cannot exceed 5 times EBITDA.**</u> If a corporation's debt is higher than that, it raises fair questions on whether or not they can service the bond. The corporation may be insolvent soon. At the time of this writing, I only buy corporate bonds paying a yield over 9%. Investing in B-rated bonds is considered risky to some but I can afford to take the risk.

Mutual funds are next. I started building my fortune with mutual funds in the middle 1990s. It was the very first investment vehicle I tried. I opened a mutual fund IRA with $1,000 and I used a dollar cost average strategy for my future purchases. I'd invest $50 a month like clockwork. Eventually, I worked up to $100 a month. As my income rose, I kept my standard of living the same and I'd invest my surplus. However, over the years, I learned mutual funds would never get me really wealthy. As the years went by, I've used my mutual funds to preserve wealth rather than build it. As with all of my investments, I've focused my mutual funds on income.

I purchase funds for yield rather than growth. I focused heavily on bond fund rather than growth funds simply because of current income. The stock funds I do own focus on high dividend yields. I cannot stress enough the focus on income. Income streams are the center of everything I do. I still spend every day, thinking of new income generating activities. I'll still write my ideas down on paper and explore them later. In my opinion, the hardest thing I've ever done is "think" and "thinking" is my most valuable skill. After looking at my present mutual fund portfolio, I notice it's a mixture of short, intermediate and long-term bonds. My money is spread evenly across maturity periods. I rest easy with these fixed dollar investments because they generate income and are heavily diversified. **I've never really had a system or rule of thumb when it comes to picking mutual funds. I've just focused on present and past income and diversification.** I'm not looking for any mutual fund to make me wealthy. I think other types of investments are much more appropriate for that. I just want my funds to preserve my wealth in down markets and so far, a portfolio focused on money market and bond funds has done that for me. **It's very important to note, I haven't purchased a mutual fund in years.** At the time of this writing, I have about $250,000 in various funds. I let the dividends reinvest but I haven't actually brought new shares in what feels like forever. At the time of this writing, I don't see myself ever buying any new shares of mutual funds again. In my opinion, mutual funds are a good investment for the right person. I think funds are perfect for passive investors. I'm a very active investor. I'm a strategy driven, process driven investor seeking significant return of capital. At the time of this writing, I believe I'll never add any of my money to mutual funds and I'll seek high risk assets with greater potential return. I'll look to buy assets like real estate, individual stocks, corporate bonds and master limited partnerships (MLPs).

I have to say a few words about master limited partnerships (MLPs). MLPs are normally sold in units. In my mind, these are cool investments because I'm kind of like a silent partner. I put up some money while someone else runs the business.

I'll get a piece of the pie for some money. Periodically, I'll get a check or a deposit in my bank account. In my experience, MLPs are pass-through entities. The way I understand it, is they avoid double taxation because the partnership isn't taxed. All income is passed-through to the partners. The way I see it, the tax advantages are huge and more powerful than any individual stock I can own. I know MLPs have complicated my taxes though. **Once I started buying MLPs, I started getting a form called Schedule K-1.** This was an incredible difficult form for me to figure out. However, with tons of Google searches and reading, I got through it. My MLPs have paid me huge amounts of income over the years. Like clockwork, the deposits come regularly. At the present time, I screen MLPs paying dividends over 9% and then I do my due diligence. If a dividend is less than 9%, it's really not worth my time unless there is an opportunity for some serious dividend growth in the near future.

Chapter 3

Perhaps nothing is more near and dear to me than real estate. I cannot say enough about its power as an investment. Since the beginning of time, it's always been a powerful investment. Real estate is the foundation of all things. Real estate grows our food and, when improved, protects us from the weather. We mine real estate for elements to produce our computers, cell phones and other electronics. We extract oil from land and feed our livestock on its open plains. We extract water from underground aquifers allowing us to bathe, cook, clean and drink. Real estate is the foundation of everything. It is the basis of all things and it's absolutely critical for our survival. **In my opinion, real estate is the most powerful of all investments.** When it comes to real estate, there is **scarcity**. There isn't any more than what presently exist today. There are no factories spitting out new land. As global population rises, more and more people will want real estate. It is valuable to our way of life as human beings and vital to our survival. Improved real estate protects us from nature's element and cultivated real estate nourishes our bodies. Out of every investment on the planet, I cannot think of a better one than real estate.

However, since real estate is so essential to humanity, it's susceptible to absurd valuations and bubbles. Real estate bubbles have happened in the past and they will happen again in the future. Humans herd-like mentality ensures it. **As with any investment, proper valuation of real estate is crucial.** I purchased my first rental property in 2011. It was a bad deal. I overpaid for the property but the lessons I learned from that experience are priceless. The lesson I learned from that deal went on to shape my future thoughts about all investments, regardless of type. Whether it's a stock, bond, mutual fund or rental property, I know now that everything must brought below market value to reduce downside risk.

I know I cannot buy a good investment at market value. It needs to be below market value and even under those conditions, it never eliminates risk. I've learned over time, I can only afford to invest and risk money I can safely lose. **There are no sure thing investments. I know I can lose 100% of my principal every time I pull the trigger and buy something.** Whether it's a property for $50,000 or a $1,000 worth of shares of some stock, I can lose it all if I am wrong.

Despite my experience, I know I'll never have a perfect batting average. I'll always swing and miss from time to time. There are just too many variable and unknowns when it comes to investing. **An important rule of thumb for me is**

nvest small amounts I can completely lose. By following this rule, I can stay focused on my long-term strategy during down markets. It's easier to let a good story develop if only 1% of your net worth is tied up in the stock, bond or real estate asset. The funny thing I've found out is over time, my definition of "small" has changed. When I first started investing, I considered $50 a small amount of money. Now, my definition of small is $1000. I have to wonder what "small" will mean to me 10 years from now.

Now, getting back to real estate, I know there is still a threat of losing 100% of my principal if I choose my real estate asset incorrectly. The dollars are much bigger when I deal with real estate and my potential for loss is greater. I know I need to be careful. Despite the risk, I've never shied away from real estate. I know it's different from every other investment on this planet. It's tangible. I can reach out and touch it. A mutual fund is a collection of stock shares. The funny thing is I've never actually seen my stock shares. Real estate isn't like that. It's easy to find. I can drive by it when I want.

I've found real estate has helped me minimize my taxation. It seems like everything is deductible; cleaning, repairs, legal expenses, property taxes, lawn care and so on. I never fully understood why the government favors real estate investors so much. I figure the government realizes it's the foundation of the economy. New technology like social media is cool but it can come and go. That gadget or website may be hot today but ultimately, it's not a necessary. Real estate is lasting wealth. I'm talking generations upon generations. Humanity will always, always need land to survive. Let's be frank, no one's survival is dependent on a cell phone. The magic of real estate never ceases to amaze me. I think about how a single real estate purchase affects my local economy. I think about one of my best purchases. I brought a property worth over $80,000 for $35,000. Just after closing, I hired an independent contractor to demo the floors and lay new ceramic tile, paint the interior, refinish the cabinets throughout, install light fixtures, ceiling fans, a new counter kitchen top, a bathroom vanity and a new kitchen backsplash. I hired him to paint the exterior too. I hired an electrician to install new outlets and light switches. I hired a plumber to install a new shower diverter. When I think about that purchase, I hired three contractors and injected about $15,000 into my local economy in about four weeks. One of the contractors hired a subcontractor to help him so actually four people went to work. I put money in their pocket permitting them to pay their living expenses. I imagine they paid rent to someone, purchased gas for their truck, ate at a local fast food place for lunch. Perhaps they brought some groceries for their family at a local market. The money they spent was someone's income. If I let my imagination run wild, I can imagine the local fast food place flush with new business having to hire new cashiers and servers. The cycle of spending and economic growth rolls on and real estate is at the tip of the spear. Here is the most curious thing I've learned about real estate. The money I spend on it never really disappears.

It grows in almost magical and mythical ways that I cannot explain. When I think about that piece of real estate I brought. I paid $35,000 and I put $15,000 into it. I could have immediately listed it and sold it for $80,000 if I wanted. I would have gotten everything I put into back and then some. Even though I decided to keep it, it still produces in a magical way through income. At the time of this writing, I've owned that property a little over a year and it's produced over $13,000 gross revenue. It isn't profitable yet but it's almost there. **Real estate is like that. It is a long-term investment and it isn't a get rich quick scheme. I had to learn this fact on my own. Financial gurus and real estate brokers never told me this fact.** I'm learning a lot more as I go on. I've learned buying a piece of real estate is like marrying someone. It's easy to get in but hard to get out. **I've learned every year I can depreciate real estate and I've found out you have to pay back that depreciation when you sell. It's called recapture depreciation.** This is something else that real estate wizards will rarely mention. I'm learning it is probably in my descendants' best interest to never sell the real estate outright. **I hope they'll do something called a 1031 exchange and keep trading up to new and better properties.** It is little secrets like this that I learned through my experiences: the good, the bad and the ugly.

In my mind, one of the greatest benefits of real estate is control. Other investment has severe limitations in this area. When I think of my stock shares, I'm technically a part owner of a company. However, unless I own significant shares, I have no power to influence how the business is run. If I own a few shares of a retail store and I feel they are charging too much for a candy bar, I can't change the price. As a hands-on investor, this is a major weakness for me. With stocks I read reports and evaluate strategies of others but I can't implement my own ideas. I have never been fully satisfied with that reality. It was never good enough. I needed more control. With real estate, I got that.

When I first started, I used a property management company. I always set the price of the rent myself. After a while, I started coordinating my own maintenance. As time passed, I began to do everything myself and I moved my properties from the partial control of others to my total control. From annual budgets to website design, I control it all now and I'm happier now. I understand some may not want that type of control and that's fine. However, for me, control is essential. I will not blindly turn over my asset and money to others and trust they will manage it correctly for me. I do have money in stocks and mutual funds but you'll find out later, it's a small percentage compared to my real estate holdings. **Stocks, bonds, mutual funds are just financial tools to me. My business is renting residential real estate.** Make no mistake about it. In my earlier books, I thought the key to managing large amounts of real estate was a good property manager. I don't think that now. The key to success is learning and doing my own property management and building my own small business around a foundation of carefully selected rental properties. For me, this approach has been more financially and personally rewarding. I know if I build a small business that I personally own, I will leave a legacy behind. My descendants for generations will know my name. My great grandfather passed down 120 acres of farmland down to his children. My grandmother received oil and mineral checks from his estate until she died. My mother still receives oil/mineral checks today. Everyone still talks about my great grandfather today. Everyone still remembers his name. I want to be remembered like that more than anything.

Another lesson I've learned is real estate lasts and produces income a long time. My oldest property was built in 1962. It is still producing income to this day. This property sends me a check every month. This property is currently 56 years old and it still produces income like clockwork. **If properly maintained real estate can last and produce income for generations. This is a key advantage to it.** My mother owns mineral rights to land in Oklahoma. It's been three generations from the original owner and the checks keep coming. In theory, other investments can work like that too. There are a few corporations that have been around 100 years or so. I suppose it comes down to what makes me comfortable and I'm more comfortable with the control that real estate offers. I firmly believe technology will never replace real estate either. I'm not certain I believe that with corporations; even if they've been around a long time.

Over the years, I learned real estate holds value better than any investment I can think of. Corporate bonds are a close second. Stocks are the worst. One day they are up. Another day they are down. Over time, the swings between stock highs and lows can be remarkable. In my own stock/mutual fund portfolio, I once had paper losses of over $10,000 overnight. Real estate does not swing like this. Its volume is too low for that. There aren't millions and millions of pieces of real estate shares changing hands every day. It sells in parcels and supply is very limited. New shares of a corporation can be printed on a whim. No one can "print" new land. It simply isn't possible. The supply of real estate is stable. Demand is usually stable so real estate normally holds value. Bubbles can and do happen but I learned real estate markets normalize rather quickly and are more stable than other markets. I think if anyone independently researches this by tracking national home sales over time, they'll come to this same conclusion. I found real estate values grow slight ahead of inflation and that is a good thing. In my market, real estate values only change a few percentage points a year. I could load the next couple of pages with graphs and table confirming my thoughts but why should I? These are just my thoughts and I'm having a conversation with a friend over coffee right…

When I purchase real estate, I try to purchase it at least $25,000 below market value. This rule of thumb helps me at least break even if I incorrectly estimate renovation expenses. It limits my risk significantly. I purchase real estate from every source I possibly can. I buy from Craigslist, Zillow, Realtor.com, VA.gov, real estate agents and courthouse steps. I've gotten some of my best deals from real estate wholesalers. Real estate wholesalers are an incredible resource for me. They do the hard work of running down deals so I don't have to.

In my mind, there isn't a specific type of real estate I avoid. Everything depends on sell price. I will buy any type of real estate at the right price. This includes single family homes, duplexes, townhouses, condos, 4-plexes or commercial property. I know certain investors stick to a single type; I'm not like that. Valuation is most important thing to me. Cap rates matter. Cash flow numbers matter. The type of asset doesn't matter to me. **I still have a major fondness for single family homes with 3 bedrooms and a two-car garage. Why? I find tenants tend to stay in these properties longer.** They tend to make these properties home. I have lower turn-over and less stress since a long-term tenant means long-term rent payments. Lately, I've developed a fondness for 2-bedroom townhouses with a garage. In my area, I never seem to have a problem renting these buildings. The rent price point is perfect to appeal to the mass market while the floor plans have just enough amenities to appeal to modern tastes.

When it comes to real estate, everything is public record. It is easy to find a lot of data about a property. I always go to my county clerk website to find data. I can find information about tax appraised value, deed history, zoning and more. I use the tax appraised value to give me a starting point for figuring out market value. Sometimes it's way off but sometimes it is spot-on. I use tax appraised value with market list price from real estate agents to arrive at true value.

I'm often asked how I estimate expenses. I do not use a complicated method. Anyone can use my method. It just requires basic math. Here is how I do it. Let us suppose current interest rate for an investment property is 4%. Let us suppose the property I want to buy is $50,000 and it rents for $850 a month. Here's how I do my numbers.

Interest rate: 4%
Principal: 1.2%
Maintenance, Repairs and Capital Investment: 2.5%
Taxes/Insurance: 2.5%

If I add all of the above numbers, I get 10.2%. I multiply this number by the property value and I get $5,100. This is my estimated annual expenses. Now, I multiply $850 by 12 to get my annual income of $10,200. Next, I multiple that figure by my expected vacancy rate. For this example, I'll use 8%. I come up with $816. I finally I put it all together with simple subtraction.

$10,200	Gross Income
- $5,100	Estimated Expenses (principal, interest, taxes, insurance, repairs, capital investment, etc.)
-$816	Vacancy Loss
$4,284	Annual Net Income
+$357	Monthly Income

This is my simple method for estimating cash flow on a potential investment property. I do not recommend anything I do. This is my method and it works for me. It is not 100% accurate nor all-inclusive. It has its limitations. Maintenance, repairs and capital investment costs do not always equal 2.5%. Some years I have spent much more on a property. Especially when it comes to capital expenditures. Once, I replaced a roof and an air conditioning system in the same year. I busted my capital expenditure budget for that particular year easily. Some years, I've had evictions. Some years I've needed to replace a roof. Some years I replaced my central heat and air conditioning system. When I had major expenses such as these my numbers go right out the window. However, overall, I have great success using this simple method for calculating gross income, expenses, vacancy loss and net income. I do not build property management expense into my numbers. There is a reason for that. I never use property management anymore. I learned management is an unnecessary expense that reduces cash flow, limits growth and my wealth. In my eyes, all I did was make someone else richer by using professional property management. **I'll never use a property manager again. In my opinion, real**

estate is not a passive investment. It is very active requiring me to get my hands dirty if I'm going to be really successful.

I think if a person doesn't want to be actively involved, they should think about getting into another business and stay away from real estate investing. I know real estate brokers will passionately disagree with me. I know some investors will too. I hope they understand that this is just my own thoughts, experiences and opinions. I don't need nor want everyone to agree with me. I don't need or want everyone to do the things I do. This book isn't written for any real estate professional or anyone for that matter; it's written for me. It is time I set the record straight and capture my thoughts, experiences and opinions before I run out of time. I'm getting older by the day and my thoughts on real estate and other financial instruments have changed over the years. It is time I update my thoughts in writing so everyone knows where I stand. It is time I capture my thoughts for my descendants.

When I initially dived into real estate investing. I thought key to real success was accumulating as much property as I can, turn it over to a property manager and watch monthly checks come in. I was wrong. I do not think a property manager is vital to success. **I don't think property managers are even useful. In my opinion, property management is a very expensive service with little return.** In the past, professional property management severely limited my cash flow and thus my ability to grow. At one point, I was paying 10% of my gross monthly rent to have a property manager collect a check from a tenant, take out their 10% and give me my share. I was coordinating my own maintenance and setting my own rent amount. After doing this for some time, I wondered what I was actually paying for.

Another time, I had a property sit vacant for months. I was working out of state so I could not manage this particular property myself. One weekend, after thinking about this vacancy, I decided to fly to the property and do a surprise site visit. I put my plan into motion. I flew in without any advance warning. I dropped into the property management company and demanded keys to the property. I drove there immediately. I didn't even stop for coffee. I just felt something was really wrong. I arrived at the property and opened the entry way door. I was shocked. The living room floor was covered with cockroaches. The dead bugs were everywhere. The deceased insects weren't the major problem. I expected that scene since I had the property professionally sprayed inside and out just prior to putting it on the market. The major problem was the property management company did not have the cockroaches cleaned up. They were showing my property to prospective tenants just like that. I fired this particular company right on the spot. For the record, I do not think all property management companies are as bad as this one. Do I think professional property management is worth the money? No. Over time, I learned to do everything myself. I learned tenant screening. I learned leasing. I learned work orders, accounting, book keeping and evictions. I even learned how to market my properties. I know if I set my mind to it, I can learn and do anything. By leveraging technology, I learned to do more with less. With my property management software, I'm easily managing my rentals on my own. I feel I can probably manage about 50 properties by myself. I guessing after that number, I'll need to take on a staff member. Since, I started self-managing my own properties, my monthly cash flow has increased significantly. I find I have more money to fund my lifestyle and pursue new investments. I find I have a lot more money to enjoy life. I view rental property as a business in every since of the word. As I grow my assets, I grow my business. Maybe one day, I will need a staff member. Maybe one day, I will need office space. As of right now, I'm doing absolutely fantastic working out of a home office with a desktop computer and internet access. I love this digital world we live in. It allows me to increase my productivity and accomplish more with less. I know I can't do everything by myself. I need help. I leverage outsourcing to fill in the gaps or holes in my business. I know me. I know what I'm good at. I know what I suck at. I do the things I'm good at and I outsource the things I suck at. I own 14 properties but I'm terrible at maintenance. I have always worked with my mind. I'm not any good at working with my hands so I hire independent contractors to do that kind of work for me.

When it comes to maintenance, I don't kid around with it. **I actually take care of my properties. I annually budget 1% of my property values for maintenance.** For example, if I have a $1,000,000 property portfolio, I budget $10,000 for repairs and maintenance. **I budget an additional 1.5% for capital improvements.** Capital improvements are upgrades prolonging assets useful life or repurposes assets for new uses. A brand-new roof, hot water heater or a new air conditioning system may qualify as a capital improvement. Everyone reading this book should consult the IRS or their own tax accountant to be sure. Why do I spend so much on repairs and improvements? I simply view my real estate rentals as a business. As I business I know I have to compete with other real estate businesses. I have to change and appeal to modern tastes or I will get left behind. At the time of this writing, it seems everyone wants an open floor with wood floors. It is all I ever see when I turn on HGTV. Therefore, I try to meet this demand. In doing so, I balance cost with aesthetics. I might knock out a wall that isn't load bearing and reinforce it with a thick beam or I may lay down vinyl plank flooring instead of actual wood. These methods allow me to compete but still stay within the constraints of my annual budget.

I think one of the toughest things is viewing your rentals as an actual business. I hear landlords say it's just a rental. I hate hearing that. I believe if a landlord views their investment properties as "just a rental", tenants will treat it as such and not take care of it. In order for me to become really successful, I had to view my rentals as a small business. I had to view it as a small business that would succeed or fail based on my own efforts and abilities and the systems and processes I put in place to run it. After I started viewing my rentals as a business, I noticed a lot of changes. I tightened up my accounting and I started logging all receipts in my ledger promptly. I started running monthly and annual profit/loss reports. I started to become more aware of my income and my expenditures. I learned to increased productivity and efficiency with automation, templates and standard procedures. I learned to analyze expenses and think of new ways to cut costs. **One of the simple ways I learned to cut costs was I started using the same color paint in all my rentals.** This reduced my "make-ready" repair expenses significantly. Before I used to cut pieces of drywall and take it down to my local home improvement store and have it matched. The funny thing is my paint was never mixed exactly right. I could always see touch-ups and it bothered me since I'm a perfectionist. I want everything to look flawless. With one simple change, I now use paint mixed at the factory. Every time, it is mixed to perfection right out of the bucket. I never see touch-up spots or streaks anymore. Repairing holes or drywall damage is a breeze for me now. **After being so successful with standardizing paint, I began to standardize everything.** Now I use the same light fixtures in all my rentals. Now I use the same ceiling fans. The flooring is standard now. Vanities are standard. Faucets are all standard. I use the same one in all my rentals. If you were to visit all of my rentals in a single day; you will see they look virtually identical. I stepped up standardization by using standardized cabinets, back-splashes and cabinet colors. I'm starting to standardize counter-tops so I can compete on a budget. Standardizing everything I can saves me money, time and effort. Now, as soon as the purchase contract is signed and executed, the design is already done.

Standardization saves me brain cells, dollars and gets my income-producing properties to market faster. There is nothing friendly about business. Business is tough and only the strong survive. In my business, I try hard to compete in every way possible. I offer better properties than my competitors with more amenities. I do not need all market share but I want my fair share. I know nothing is given to me. I know I need to go out there and take it and standardization gives me an edge.

Originally, I was paying a company $15 a month to advertise my rentals. **After I found out I could advertise on Zillow and Cozy for free, I started doing my marketing myself for free.** When it comes to running your own business, every dollar counts. Save anywhere, everywhere possible and invest your profits. I market my rentals on Zillow, Cozy and occasionally Facebook. I started off wasting money with boosted posts, now I find specialized groups and market there. On Facebook I'm part of real estate investor groups and several real estate rental groups in my area. This marketing has been extremely effective for me and 100% free.

As I built my real estate small business, I took time to learn how to do it correctly as I went. **For this reason alone, my real estate license has been invaluable. In my opinion, every real estate property manager or investor should get one.** I got my education online. It was very cost-effective and easy. I studied in my spare time between managing my rentals and leisure activities. Getting my real estate license was well-worth the money. The question I often get is "Do I need a real estate license?" I answer truthfully no. In Texas, you do not need a real estate license to manage your own properties but you should get one anyway. The next question I get is "Why, should I get a license?" It is a simple answer really.

I think everyone should get a license for competence. Everyone needs to operate in accordance with the law. Everyone needs to do things legally and correctly. There is no substitute for formal education. This book is not professional advice and it isn't a substitute for formal education. As I've gotten bigger, I have become a target for scammers and crooks alike. I needed accurate and current knowledge of real estate laws and procedures to deal with these threats to my small real estate empire. In addition, having my own real estate license allows me to purchase properties off the Multi-Listing Service (MLS) at a discount. I saved thousands on a single purchase by representing myself and I claim one-half of the commission. In a typical real estate transaction, the seller pays 6% in brokerage fees. Half or 3% goes to the selling broker and the other half goes to the broker bringing the buyer. When I represent myself, I keep my share of that commission. Like I said, it saves me thousands. In the past, I brought multiple times off the MLS in a given year. During those times, I saved some serious money. I can think of a lot of additional reasons why I think a real estate license is a necessity. I know the education I got gave me the knowledge and skills to fill out my own contracts. It has given me confidence to list and sell my own properties without brokerage fees. I can legally receive referral fees from other agents with a real estate license. I can represent others as a buyer's agent. I can sale new homes. I can apartment locate.

I can legally sell property for others. The list of positive reasons for getting a state real estate license is long. There are some negatives but I don't sweat the potential drawbacks. The truth is I'm an honest businessman with integrity. I'm not trying to rip anyone off so I do not fear investigations into my practices. I follow the law to the letter. **One of the greatest reasons I maintain my real estate license is it keeps me competent in the field of real estate.** For that reason alone, I plan to maintain my license as long as the Great State of Texas allows me to serve. Everyday, I see landlords and real estate investors open themselves up to lawsuits, ethic complaints, code and fair housing law violations because they aren't competent with current laws. A real estate license helps me stay smart on the industry. It keeps me competent and competency is a critical building block for integrity and honesty. In my opinion, everyone touching a piece of real estate or signing a real estate contract or form ought to have a real estate license.

My son and I had a long conversation. I told him a dirty little secret every country across the globe doesn't want him to know. I told him money isn't really valuable. It is just paper…back by…well, nothing. If anything, I guess it is backed by confident. I have to trust I can take my paper dollars to a store and trade them for goods and services. The store receiving my dollars is trusting they can use them to pay employees. The employees are trusting they can use their dollars to pay rent and so on. Honestly, paper money is just paper. It is printed on some machine, most likely at the Bureau of Engraving and Printing and it is backed by nothing. It certainly isn't backed by gold. The United States has been off the gold standard since the 70s. <u>**Since paper money depends on confidence, I choose to trade it every chance I get for real, tangible assets.**</u> Of course, my preference is real estate because land is the basis of all things and fundamental for all life. Land has real value since our survival is tied to it. The survival of all life on this planet is linked with land. Land is the real deal. If I had one moment of absolute brilliance in my life, it was the day I realized land and life are one. You cannot have life without land and because of that, there is no investment more important. There is no investment more valuable. Stocks alone never made me a millionaire. I did well but I never broke into the millionaire dollar man club until I started buying real estate. The power of real estate's leverage, income and appreciation allowed me to break into millionaire estates with great speed and efficiency. I kicked down the club's door in just a few, short years.

I want my fantastic tenants to stay. I love tenants that pay rent on-time and take care of my properties. In return, I strive to keep these tenants for a long time. Most of the time, I'm successful. How do I do it? I think it's easy. All it takes is a few simple steps. I treat them with respect. I strive for standout customer service and I invest in my properties. I'll discuss each step individually.

First, respect is key. It doesn't matter if a tenant is on government assistance or has a career, I treat all people with respect regardless of their income or bank account. Real estate is a relationship business and having fantastic relationships result in repeat business, referrals and great reviews. All of these things affect your ability to grow your business. I see landlords get really disrespectful with their tenants. They have that "if you don't do what I say, I'll throw you off my land" attitude. It is a bad attitude and it is unnecessary. I never had a problem because I inform tenants "everything is business and nothing is ever personal." It works exceptionally well so far because it is so true. I even smile at evictions because it's never personal. It's just business. My business has expenses. My business can't afford to let anyone live in a property for free. It doesn't mean I don't have a heart. My business will fail if I don't enforce leases. It is just that simple. However, I enforce leases and rules and regulations with a smile. I guess it goes back to the old saying "treat people like you want to be treated." I do this myself and it is working for me. I think it works for everyone. I imagine what the world would be like if we just treat each other with respect.

Customer service. I cannot stress the importance of treating everyone kindly. My tenants are customers. I wouldn't spend my hard-earned money in any establishment treating me poorly. Why should I expect my tenants to do the same? I recently had to send out 3-day notices. I did so with professionalism, a good attitude, empathy and kind words. It doesn't help my situation or theirs to get fired up about things. My tenants may have excuses about why they cannot pay rent or whatever but I politely tell them this is a business…and every business has bills and creditors that must be paid. I cannot give my bank excuses. I suppose I can but there is no excuse good enough to stop foreclosure on my properties. Despite all of this, I conduct business during good times and bad with an incredible attitude and a smile. Just having good customer service isn't enough for me to keep incredible tenants for a long time. I have to reward their patronage with upgrades. I have to invest in my properties.

Every year, I budget for capital improvements. I budget 1.5% of my portfolio value for capital improvements. I spend this money on upgrades so I can retain fantastic tenants, extend the life of my rentals and increase property values. When I invest in my properties, I know I'm doing the right thing for myself, my tenants, my community and my descendants. Improving property creates economic activity, increases values and extends production life of an asset. I was watching a documentary last night. It was about the LeFrak family. The LeFraks are a powerful real estate family in the New York area. They are third generation. Their wealth started with their grandfather in the early 1900s. The funny thing is the family still holds some of his initial purchases. Through renovations, they have extended useful life of the properties proving real estate, when properly maintained can produce income for generations. These examples are why I invest in my properties on a continual basis. I have no plans to ever let any of my holdings go into despair. There is a curious side effect of my habit of continuous reinvestment. I stay at 100% occupancy most of the time. I rarely have a long-term vacancy despite being in a city with a vacancy rate from 8 to 10%. Professional real estate brokerage can't duplicate my performance. The vacancy rates for the best firms sit at around 2%. Most are probably much higher. My low vacancy rates permit me to increase or maintain annual revenues. This allows more reinvestment. It is a wonderful cycle. I never intend to fall into the slumlord trap. Slumlording is a false promise. The short-term profits are good at the expense of the property and economic health of the neighborhood. Over time, unmaintained properties draw less income and attract lower quality tenants. These lower quality tenants may do more damage and wear and tear on the properties. The result is lower market rent prices and lower property values. And the vicious negative cycle continues. Eventually, slumlord are usually forced to sell at below market prices because their properties are absolute dumps. Then, an investor like me purchases the properties and invest money into them restarting the "wonderful cycle." I always invest good money in my properties on a reoccurring basis. It is good business and it is good real estate. In the end, I know this strategy will put me far ahead of the pack.

Real estate is a great investment for me. However, an even better investment was starting my own business. It just happens to be a real estate business. I initially started buying and holding my real estate assets passively. It just didn't work for me. I'm an active guy. I wanted to set my own rent prices. I wanted to do my own marketing. I wanted to run day-to-day operations, I wanted to do everything. I couldn't take it so I took my properties back from a property management company and I started to do things myself. It was the best decision I ever made. Now I do everything. I manage. I market. I maintain. Taking the plunge into my own real estate business increased my gross cash flow instantly. The most important thing I did was re-invest my profits. It was essential for growth.

As with everything, I budget capital investments. One year, I purchased a new office computer. One year, I upgraded my real estate software. One year, I purchased a foreclosure list subscription. Every year I invest some of my profits into my business in order to help it grow. Unfortunately, I got poor returns from some of my investments. I tried a pay service that boosting my rentals on social media but it didn't work for me. Once I figured out it wasn't working for me, I spent the rest of the money I budgeted for social media marketing on other things. Business is active. It is not passive. I have to think, try things…fail…try other things…fail and then eventually succeed. I know I have to stay persistent and determined. Building a business is hard. It's stressful. It is a lot of effort. However, payouts are enormous. I'm still in the early stages of making this business work but I know I can create something generational. I can create something I can pass to my descendants. Sometimes I imagine a life for my descendants much better than mine. I imagine my offspring not having to beg others for jobs. I imagine a life where the family business is waiting for them once they finish school. I imagine it for my children. I imagine it for my grandkids. That is the American dream to me. My goal is to build a foundation for something special while I am here and my dream is that my children will make it better and grow it larger. My hope is their children will grow it larger still and so on. Life isn't about working a job to me. It's about building and growing something special.

Right now, the toughest and best thing about my business is I do everything. I am in charge of accounting, book-keeping, operations, marketing, maintenance, legal and leasing. It is tough because I do everything and it gets busy sometimes. It is awesome because I do everything and I have learned so much. One day, I will have to take on additional staff. When I do, I will have worked every job at some point so I will have a clear understanding of what needs to happen in order to solve problems. I think it is in everyone's interest to build their own business. It doesn't have to be real estate, it could be in anything that interests them. Life pulled me into the direction of real estate. When I retired from the military, I imagined a life of long hours, late nights and few days off in corporate America. After looking around, I decided I didn't want that life. I decided to earn my own way. I decided to build my own business. I built a small business as a kid selling marbles once. I figured I did it then; I could do it now.

Perhaps, the most important factor in my financial success are my personal qualities. There are two things stick out to me. Number one is my lifestyle. Number two is my insatiable appetite for bargains and deals. I will talk about each one.
My lifestyle is arguably the single most important factor in my financial success. My lifestyle permits me to save capital required to put my financial plans in motion. This is America. In this country, it takes money to make money. In my early years, I worked a job like everyone else. I hesitate to call it a job. It was

more of a career. I was in the military. For me, it was the best decision in the world. In the military, I deployed to two wars and two peace-keeping operations. I traveled all around the world and met new, interesting people. I met fascinating people and I saw dire poverty, conflict and suffering. In the military, I experienced the world. It was raw and uncensored. My military service shaped who I am today. It taught me to pursue integrity, service and excellence in everything I do. Those values are my foundation today. The military not only molded me; it gave me a paycheck too. My first paycheck in early 1992 was just over $700 a month. After taxes, I cleared a little over $300 every two weeks. Now it seems like such a tiny sum. It seems so impossible to live on today. At the time, I felt like a giant though. I felt rich and loaded with money. On payday, I'd cash my check and walk around the local mall in Champaign, Illinois like a big shot. I made it rain buying my friends sodas and slices of pizza. I felt like a boss. I was making the most money I've ever seen in my life. At the beginning, I wasted it all and saved virtually nothing. My training in personal finances was non-existent. I knew absolutely nothing about budgeting, saving and investment and it showed. I blew every paycheck. I lived paycheck to paycheck. However, it didn't last long.

After a few years, I was stationed in Georgia and I met a military officer who was an astute investor. He talked to me about investing in mutual funds. He said he saved hundreds of thousands over his short lifetime investing in funds. From that point, I was hooked. I started reading everything I could on personal finance. I read book after book. In my opinion, the greatest book I ever read is "The Richest Man in Babylon." I still listen to that audio book on a regular basis today. It was that book along with "Personal Finance for Dummies" that changed my life and started me on the road leading to where I am today.

I became more responsible. I was loaded with consumer debt because I used my credit card to purchase furniture for my first apartment. I moonlighted and worked a second job as a convenience store cashier to pay off all my debts. Once, my debts were paid, I cut up my credit card and committed to paying for all my future purchases with cash. Then I focused on my career. I did everything I could to move up my career ladder and earn more money. I am a relatively smart guy so I found success. As my earnings increased, I maintained my same standard of living and pushed my excess income into mutual funds. Periodically, I still review my personal expenses and cut costs where I can. Periodically, I review my cable expenses. I look at my insurance costs. I look at my entertainment expenditures. I still put everything under the microscope from time to time. If there is any fat anywhere; I quickly trim it.

For decades, I've done this. I still do it. I have over $1.4 million in financial assets yet I do not have cable tv. I stream my favorite tv shows instead. I still do not buy new cars. I purchase all my vehicles slightly used. I rarely spent over $10,000 for a car. When I shop at grocery stores, I buy store brand products. Some may say their taste is different, I disagree. Store brand products taste the same to me. A green bean tastes like a green bean despite the label in my opinion. I bundle my insurance costs to save money. I have my auto, homeowners, life, dental and rental property insurance all under the same carrier. I still order water at restaurants instead of sodas or alcohol drinks. Water is a healthier option and it is much cheaper. I bundle my flight and hotel on travel sites like Priceline and Orbitz. I take Ubers instead of taxis. I have joined just about every restaurant rewards program there is. As my mind races, I realize that I'm getting into my second character trait. I have an insatiable appetite for deals.

I love deals. For some strange reason, I get excited when I hunt down a fantastic deal. It doesn't matter if it is a piece of real estate or saving 50% off a meal in a restaurant; I get insanely excited about finding deals. It is a personal characteristic of mine. I love hunting down deals and I strive to never pay full price for anything. For example, I only upgrade my electronics on Black Friday.

Deal hunting is easy in the digital age too. I have all the major companies I do business with email me their promotions right to my inbox. Home Depot, Walmart, Vista Print, Priceline, Sam's Club and Orbitz are all sending me periodic promotions. I Groupon my entertainment needs. Restaurants are the same way. They email me promotions weekly. Whenever I get ready to spend money, I just have to pick the promotion and place. There is a market price for everything and I never intend to pay that price. Regardless of good or service, I strive to pay below market prices. I shop at discount stores like Big Lots, Ross and Burlington Coat Factory. Often, I'll buy my long-sleeve shirts from Sam's Club or Walmart. I look like a million bucks and I drive a luxury car and I've done it at bargain prices. Not only do I look like I have a million bucks; I actually do.

What has been the result of my lifestyle and character traits? I've built a small fortune plus I realized a dramatic improvement to quality of life. Honestly, I can eat out every day of the week now with no trouble. I can travel when and where I want. If I was into shopping, I could do that regularly too. Fortunately, I'm not. I like to spend my money on experiences and I have new experiences regularly. I frequent vineyards all over the state. Visiting restaurants with exotic foods are a favorite pastime of mine. Ethiopian, Greek, Hungarian, Indian, Chinese, Thai are all some of my favorite cuisines. And I regularly indulge. I love music concerts and dinner shows. Live theater is fun to me. As a result of my deal hunting and humble lifestyle I'm able to enjoy all of my favorite pastimes on demand. I save every dollar I can because every dollar counts in this game of life and finance.

Chapter 4

Like my other books, this is a short read. In my opinion, this book has more meat and potatoes than my others because I share more of my experiences and I answer specific questions about how I arrived at this point in my life.

The following pages consist of questions I've been asked in the past. For readers curious about how I arrived at this point, I'm certain they will find my answers very valuable. As I said, I think even seasoned investors will find nuggets in the following pages.

These are my own personal thoughts and opinions and I do not recommend anything I do. Everyone should develop their own investing style. Everyone should develop their own systems and processes. Everyone should find the tactics, tools and procedures that works for them in their own market. Experience will always be your best teacher.

I hope you enjoy the following Q&A session below; I know I enjoyed writing it.

Question 1: I've often thought of investing in real estate. I presently don't have any money or credit. How did you get started?

Answer: I started off in a similar situation. I had no money or credit. I focused on my personal finances first. I paid off my debt. I started saving to build a nest egg. Next, I worked to increase my credit score. As my credit score increased, I found it easier to qualify for loans and got better terms too. Once I became credit worthy and I had enough saved, I purchased my first home and the rest is history. One home becomes two. Two becomes three. The one thing I've done over the years is not grow to fast. I've always understood borrowed money must be paid back at some point so keeping a comfortable and manageable debt load is important to me.

Question 2: I want to get started in real estate. Did you find a real estate license necessary?

Answer: For me, a real estate license is invaluable. Let me explain why. A real estate license provides me with vital technical knowledge of the real estate business. I learned everything from school. I learnt contracts, easements, zoning, deeds and much more. Anyone getting into this business needs to be competent on all those topics and then some. In school, I studied how to estimate the value of property; a critical skill. I found a real estate license was inexpensive. I think I only paid about $400 for online training when I went in 2016. It is inexpensive to carry the license too. At the time of this writing, it only costs $110 to renew your license every two years in Texas. Even if an investor doesn't ever intend to work actively in real estate; a license makes sense to me for the knowledge. Every two years, there is continuation training requirements levied by the state. The continuation training forces me to stay current and up-to-date with changes in law and code. For me, my license has kept me abreast with changes in laws for property management, contracts and wholesaling. Contrary to what many believe, there are state laws covering wholesaling. It is not a fully unregulated industry. There are financial benefits for having a real estate license too. When my license is active, I represent myself as a real estate agent in my own purchases and I get a 3% discount on any property I purchase off the Multi-Listing Service (MLS). If I buy a single property a year off the MLS; my license more than pays for itself. Having a license opens doors for me. If I make my license active, I can actually work in property management for a real estate brokerage if I want or I can take listings or represent buyers. Having an active real estate license opens many doors to many income producing activities. I can manage properties for others too. There are a bunch of things I can do with an active real estate license. It is a powerful tool for your business.

Question 3: When it comes to your real estate license, what school did you attend?

Answer: I went to the Austin Institute of Real Estate in Austin, Texas in 2016. I took online course. In my opinion, it was a great education and well worth the money. The school recently changed its name to the **Real Estate Business School**. I still take my continuing education requirement through the school.

Question 4: How do you find fantastic deals?

Answer: Aside from free websites like Zillow and Realtor.com, I subscribe to a paid source as well. **I purchase an annual subscription to RealtyTrac.com**. At the time of this writing, it costs me $200 a year and it is well worth it! The big thing is RealtyTrac provides a frequently updated listing of properties in the process of foreclosure and headed to auction. I can send these owners a postcard if I want and offer to purchase their property before foreclosure. This saves property owners from wrecking their credit and I just might get a fantastic deal too. Another possible way to take advantage of this situation and create mutual benefit for both parties is offering to list their property on the MLS. When my license is active, this creates another income stream for me too. The measly $200 a year is well-worth the price of this service. RealtyTrac pulls data for the Veterans Administration (VA) website too. The VA is an incredible source of foreclosures. I have brought plenty of property from the VA over the years. Although, it may seem hard to believe, I have found incredible deals off of Craigslist too. Most real estate wholesalers post on Craigslist. I have seen extremely motivated private owners post there too. You can find some great deals on Craigslist. I surf both of these websites daily looking for deals. I have found the Multi-Listing Service great too.

Another thing I've done is go through public property tax records and send out-of-state real estate owners postcards offering to purchase their properties. I help them out by cashing out a property fast and they help me out by giving me a deal. The important thing is I disclose everything. I disclose I have a real estate license and I disclosure I may sell or rent this property for a profit. It is important for anyone operating in this business to conduct themselves with integrity and honesty. Landlording isn't easy when you live in the same city as your property. In my opinion, it is virtually impossible when you are out of state. Absentee owners open themselves up for getting taken advantage of. In my experience, I have seen these absentee owners get raked over the coals. I have seen these owners get juiced for their slim monthly profits by unnecessary inspection and marketing fees. I have seen poor screening by property management companies resulting in frequent turnover and expensive property damage. Heck, I have lived it myself. I used to have property managers. Now I do everything myself. In my opinion, real estate isn't a passive activity. Owners need to be hands-on or invest in a Real estate Investment Trust (REIT) instead. Getting back to question, I have found some absentee owners are anxious to sell. Low to negative profit margins and substandard property management are the root cause. These property owners find real estate isn't as profitable and passive as real estate gurus on late-night tv infomercials led them to believe.

Question 5: What about borrowing money? Do you use hard money or private money? Do you use traditional banks? How do you get your money?

Answer: I do not use private or hard money. In my opinion, I think it is too expensive. I use my local community bank. I go through commercial lending departments. My bank is called **Extraco Banks** in case anyone is wondering. I have always had great credit and I've always been a fantastic money manager once I learned how to do it. When I first called Extraco Banks, I set up a meeting with

VP of Commercial Lending and I briefed the gentleman on my business plan. I took in a paper copy and I went over it line by line. I also took in a balance sheet I created with Excel and I covered my present assets and liabilities. We discussed my resume, my education and current experience with real estate. He liked me. He liked what I said and since then I've had no problem with funding. If I need money, I just email him or his assistant and it is there. I have found it critically important to maintain my credit worthiness. I get money on the cheapest terms available. In my experience, national lenders have too much regulation holding them back from making loans. At the time of this writing, a borrower cannot have more than 6 active loans with most of them. I suppose this is due to Dodd-Frank regulations. I'm not sure but that is my guess. For some reason, I find community banks have more freedom to assume risk and lend. Maybe it is because they aren't selling these loans on the secondary market; I don't know. The one thing I know is I'm grateful for my community bank's ability to lend me money. I couldn't grow without it. I wouldn't be where I am today.

Question 6: I noticed you worked in a local real estate brokerage. Did you find that useful?

Answer: I found that incredibly useful. I cannot stress how important that was for me. I learnt a lot about contracts in school but nothing compares to hands-on activity. I didn't feel really comfortable until I was actually filling out real contracts. I kept my eyes open too. I learned about property management and marketing. I attended evictions and I learnt how to handle legal matters like lawsuits. I only stayed in a brokerage working for someone else for six months but I learned a ton in six months. I don't think I would be where I am today without that experience.

Question 7: How do you feel about guru courses? Have you ever attended one?

Answer: I never attended a guru course. I attended a real estate expo once because I was really curious. I got a cheap ticket on Groupon and I had nothing to do that Saturday so I decided to go for some entertainment. As I suspected, I found it to be a pitch fest with little useful information. The salesmen came at me from the start, promising big returns and financial freedom. Of course, there were plenty of stories of retiring early and all that mess. I sat there for about four hours getting nothing useful. At that point, I left early. I believe there was another 4 hours left on the schedule. I just couldn't take it anymore. I believe real estate is market dependent and I think knowing your market is key to success. I do not feel I could get what I needed from any course or book. From the best books, I got general knowledge at best. I got the most from getting my real estate license and being active in my local real estate market. In my market, I need to know what is a good value. I need to know what is over-priced. I need to know tenants too. I need to know if I can get away with a laminate countertop in this area or if tenants demand granite. These things are being an expert in a real estate market and a real estate market varies by location. In my opinion, the only way to really know a real estate market is to live in it and actively work in it. It is another reason I don't own property out of my area. I need to be in a comfortable driving distance for me to buy and hold.

Question 8: What about online real estate message groups? Have you found these tools useful?

Answer: I think the average person needs to be very careful online. I seen a ton of new investors get ripped off. **There are a lot of predators online.** They promise unbelievable results from wholesaler courses. The offer books and podcasts for fees. There are a lot of ways a new investor can lose their hard-earned cash online. I post on a few message boards from time to time. I mostly just offer encouragement or sympathy. I don't offer any advice, legal or otherwise. I read these boards largely for entertainment and periodically I post a link to my website. Who knows, I may get a real estate deal off a message board one day. When I was in sales, I posted more often and I found clients from time to time off message boards. It can be a good place to find investors but overall, I feel like a newbie shouldn't trust anything they see online. There are too many people ripping folks off on the internet in my opinion.

Question 9: Where did you find your real estate mentor?

Answer: I think the worst place to find a mentor is online. Years ago, I found a mentor in the real estate industry. I was buying property as an investor and my real estate broker was an investor too. I was just starting out. He was much bigger. I think at the time, he owned close to 30 rental properties. Over causal conversation, I learnt things about different topics in the industry and my local real estate market. I agreed with some of his thoughts and I disagreed with others. Over time, I developed my own style but those conversation were useful. If I were starting out now, **I'd probably attend a local real estate investor group off Meetup.com or attend monthly real estate auctions off the courthouse steps.** I find serious and most knowledgeable real estate investors attend auctions. If I was just starting out, I'd go there regularly, be social and hope to get lucky. In my area most serious real estate investors are brokers too. One might get a mentor and a job as a real estate agent at the same time, if they are lucky.

Question 10: Have you ever used owner financing or offered owner financing on your properties?

Answer: I never used owner financing. I'd probably be open to it as a buyer but I haven't ever seen lending terms that make sense. At the time of this writing, I have a 775 credit score so I get fantastic terms through my local bank. I never offered owner financing either. In my market, the folks offering owner financing are usually trying to sell property in severely depressed and undesirable zip codes. I don't own any properties in those areas and I really don't have any intention of buying in those areas unless I get an incredible deal. Therefore, I haven't had an opportunity to offer owner financing. I understand owner financing can be a powerful tool to make money and offer a service to those who don't quality for traditional financing but I never used it personally.

Question 11: How did you setup your business? LLC or sole proprietorship?

Answer: I love simplicity so I went with a sole proprietorship. Although, it doesn't offer legal protections like an LLC, I'm not worried about it. I don't fear lawsuits because I operate ethically, honesty and in accordance with the law. Since that is the case, a sole proprietorship works fine for me. **I find lenders lend more freely to a sole proprietorship since all assets are fair game in the event of a default.** I'm fine with that too. If a lender lends me money; they will get paid back. I always pay my debts. I seen LLCs not offer the legal protections that owners think either. I know a guy who personally got sued for a security deposit despite the property being held under an LLC. Unless I get significantly bigger; a sole proprietorship works for me for the time being.

Question 12: How many rentals do you currently have? What kind of property management software do you use?

Answer: I have 14 properties, 12 rentals, one unimproved piece of land and my personal home. I use **LandlordMax property management software**. When I purchased it a couple of years ago, I think I paid a flat fee between $200-$300. After trying other software out there, I found this one was the easiest to use. It definitely allowed me to grow my business and manage it efficiently. With this software, I'm guessing I could manage about 50 properties without taking on any additional staff. It simplifies everything for me. Accounting, operations, maintenance, book-keeping; you name it. This software gave me the confidence to self-manage and grow.

Question 13. What about those ads in Craigslist offering real estate investor trainee jobs paying $10,000? Do you know anything about those?

Answer: I don't know much about those advertisements. I seen handwritten bandit signs on street corners advertising the same thing too. For the life of me, I cannot believe any business offering a $10,000 a month trainee job would use bandit signs. I think they are trying to sell folks some sort of course or something. If that is the case, new investors would do much better going to a legitimate real estate school and getting their real estate license. It will likely be a much better education and a lot cheaper too.

Question 14. Do you self-manage or use a property manager?

Answer: I brought my first investment property in 2011. I started off using a property manager to manage it for me. It was a terrible experience. My property was renovated, fairly priced and it sat vacant. In fact, it was vacant for months. I think it was about 3 months actually. I was out of state, working in Virginia and my investment property was in Texas. For the life of me, I couldn't understand why my property was vacant. On a whim, I took some time off from my job and flew back unannounced to Texas to inspect the property. I flew in on a Sunday evening, the following morning, I marched into the property management company and politely insisted they hand over the keys so I could walk through my rental. What I found made me furious! There were dead cockroaches all over my property. That was ok because I treated the property for pests before I left. However, what wasn't ok was the property management company was showing my property to prospective tenants with dead insects littered across the floor. It gave the appearance the property was infested but it actually was pest-free. The bugs were all dead. I'm not going to lie, I was pissed. I stomped into the property management company and fire them on the spot. They said I needed to terminate in writing as written in the contract. I looked around and grabbed a napkin and scribbled "I'm taking my property back immediately – Kevin McNeely" and that was that. As a property owner, I know I have a lot of power. I know property management companies need me more than I need them. When I did use a property management company, I paid well-under the standard 10% commission rate. Why? Because I knew I was coming from a position of power. They need my property. Without my property, they don't have income. Without income, they can't pay their bills. I wish more property owners understood this point.

They would be better negotiators if they understood who has the position of power before they enter a negotiation. At this point in my life, I don't ever see myself using a property management company again. If I get really large, my own business will grow with my rentals. I think the secret to real multi-generational wealth is ownership of land and land improvements.

Question 15. Can you expand on that statement? Ownership?

Answer: In my opinion, real estate is the foundation of all things. Everything comes from it, that is why it is so valuable. That is why it's been so valuable since humans invented land rights. It only makes sense to me that real estate is the bedrock of my portfolio of assets. You have to own real estate. It makes no sense to me to own a business but not own the building and the land a business operates on. Owning a business without owning the land is just working a job to me. There is no opportunity to build that next McDonald's without owning the land and building. Ray Kroc, the founder of McDonald's finally figured that out. Once he did, his business had explosive growth and his power to influence people and events grew. Ownership of asset matter, it is the only way to cure income inequality. It must be long-term ownership of assets. When I buy an asset, I have the intention of never selling it. I'm careful how much I pay for assets and I always keep a lot of cash in my accounts. Why? In business, things come up and I never want to jeopardize my business or my assets. Businesses have expenses, sometimes unexpected expenses. I have to have money ready to deal with these situations. In the rental business, sometimes an air conditioning system goes out. Replacing an air conditioning system isn't cheap. I need money ready to deal with that situation. There is another reason I hoard cash. Opportunities pop up out of nowhere. Sometimes I'm sitting in my home office with nothing on my schedule, I get a phone call or receive an email and my whole day changes. I go out to see a property. If it looks good, I write up contracts that day. On the following day, money is at the title company and the property is under contract. But getting back to the original question, ownership of tangible assets is the way to go. Intangible assets like stocks are fine too. Tangible is better in my opinion but intangible is ok. With all assets, I buy and hold them for the long-term. I expect to do really well using that strategy.

Question 15. If you never plan on selling an asset, what do you do when an asset is past its operational life? For example, what happens when a floor plan just doesn't work anymore and you can't remodel the property to make it work?

Answer: For the most part, I can extend the life of a property with remodels for a long-time but it is possible that contemporary tastes change so much; remodeling doesn't help. In these situations, I will sell the asset. However, I am very mindful of this thing called recapture depreciation. In order to avoid paying any recapture depreciation taxes, I plan to sell my older rentals when they near the bottom of their operational life and purchase either larger properties with more doors or newer construction. **The process is called a 1031 exchange.** I think all real estate investors should learn about 1031 exchanges. Well, that is my plan. I'm going to use 1031 exchanges when I divest old assets but I haven't had to execute it yet but that's my plan.

Question 16. Is there any type of property you avoid? Do you invest in everything? Single-family, multi-family and commercial?

Answer: I like to say I would invest in all types of property. Right now, I own townhouses and single-family homes. I'm definitely open to all other types, I just haven't found a deal that made financial sense to me yet. In my opinion, it is better to wait for a deal rather than overpay for something. I invest in all areas too; at the price right. I invest in severely distressed areas. I would invest in wealthy areas. It all depends on sale price of the property relative to market value. No zip code is off limits for me. When I first started, I was scared to invest in economically depressed areas. Later I realized some of the highest profit margins are in these areas. Property management might be more challenging but if I keep my property management operations calendar-driven, process driven, I know I won't have much of a problem.

Question 17. What does that mean? Calendar-driven, process-driven property management?

Answer: Calendar-driven, process-driven property management is something I developed for me. I needed a way to take my emotions out of property management and operate my rentals more like a business. I figured that out using a calendar-driven, process-driven approach. Here is how I actually run my property management. Rent is due on the 1st. On the 3rd, a reminder that the rent isn't paid goes out. At the end of the day on the 5th, a late fee of $25 is charged. On the 6th, 3 day notices go out. On the 18th, I file for eviction at the Justice of the Peace. Every event is driven by the calendar and every event has a process tied to it. This calendar driven process is applied to all residents regardless of color, national origin, income, religion or whatever. Nothing stops the calendar driven process. If a car breaks down, it doesn't matter, a 3 day notice still goes out on the

6th regardless. Medical issues, the calendar dates still apply. My rentals are a business and I operate it like one. I can't think of any excuse that my bank will accept; I have to pay my mortgage regardless of the circumstance. I can't say to the bank "I'll pay you when my tenant pays me." It doesn't work like that. The rentals are a business and my business has bills.

Question 18. What about real estate forms like a lease? Where did you get those?

Answer: **I got all my legal forms from Nolo**. I brought the landlord package and it is fantastic. There is virtually a form for everything. I can't remember how much I paid but I know it was under a $100. It came with a legal guide too. Occasionally, I will need a form that isn't available in the package. When that is the case, I usually search out that single form on the internet. The forms usually come with an electronic version so after I buy it, I add it to my library.

Question 19. How do you know if you are following the law and doing things correctly?

Answer: **Texas Property Code is my go-to reference**. I'm always in it. I'm either reading about things affecting my present situation or learning about things that may affect my situation. I think every state has a state code that governs real estate and residential tenancies. I live and operate in Texas so I follow their code.

Question 20. It seems like there are a lot of legal requirements. Has anyone ever threatened to sue you?

Answer: As I get bigger there always seems to be some new person wanting me to cut them a quick check for this or that. I do thing stringently by Texas Property Code so I know I am right and I do not stress over baseless threats. I answer these frivolous legal threats and I don't back down either. I always answer legal threats formally and in writing. I carefully highlight references from Texas Property Code that support my position. If it comes to litigation, I'd happily plead my case before a judge. I do not understand why people fear civil court so much. Civil court is a place where people go before a judge to work out their disagreements. It is a civilized way to reach a resolution. If I need to go to court, I'll go with a smile. I will stick to the facts and keep my emotions out of it.

Question 21. How do you keep your emotions out of it?

Answer: I view my rentals as a business. Every business has its up and downs. Every business has its profitable quarters and every business has periods where it suffers a loss. People steal from retail businesses all the time. People steal from me by not paying rent. It is just the price of being in this business. Things will not run perfectly every day. If a tenant doesn't pay rent, I'm very polite with them and I politely conduct my calendar-driven process.

Question 22. I know you purchase your own properties without a real estate agent. Is it hard to do?

Answer: I don't think so. For me, the process is relatively simple. I find a property I want to buy. Once the seller and I agree to terms and valuation, **I fill out the purchase contracts available on the Texas Real Estate Commission's website.** The forms are free for anyone to use however, there is a declaimer on the website saying the forms are intended for real estate professionals and if parties choose to use the forms on their own, they assume all risks. I'm paraphrasing but it is something like that. So getting back to my purchase process, I find the property. I fill out the TREC contracts. Then, I take the contracts with the earnest money to the title company and that's that. From that point, the title company clears the title, receives all the funds and ensures everyone gets paid and the property transfers to the new owner. In my opinion, the title company does all the work.

Question 23. I hear there is a really high vacancy rate in your city. However, your occupancy is currently at 100%. How do you keep your rentals filled?

Answer: First, I view my rentals as a business and I feel like I'm in competition with every rental on my block. When I have a vacancy, I go to Zillow and Realtor.com and I check the monthly rental rates of all rentals near mine. Next, I flip through the photos and I see what their rentals are bringing to the table. I'm checking the kitchen countertop age and type. I'm looking at the carpet's color and condition. I'm evaluating ceiling fans and light fixtures. Paint. Everything. If my rental looks better, I immediately put it on the market. If it doesn't I use some of my capital improvement budget and I upgrade some things. Then I undercut their price. You see most investors are using a property manager so they have additional expenses I don't have. I can beat them every time on price and aesthetics. I can put to market a better value than my competitors. After I have my design and market price rent figured out. I put my listing on **Zillow** and **Realtor.com**. I will throw it on **Craigslist** and **FaceBook** too. On FaceBook, I'm part of a Killeen Rentals group. It is a group designed for renters looking for private owners. I feel my highest quality applicants come from **Zillow**. The Department of Housing and Urban Development estimated Killeen's vacancy rate at 10.8% in 2017 but I haven't had any problems using my strategy. I'm not worried about it either. Like I said, since I self-manage, my competitors will never be able to compete with me on price.

Question 24. How did you buy your first rental?

Answer: I brought my first rental with cash in 2011. I remember it vividly. I overpaid for that property too. Later, I became more comfortable with debt so I borrowed against the property using what is called a cash-out refinance or simply a cash-out refi. The bank allowed me to cash-out 80% of the property's value. As I recall it, the property assessed at about $56,000 so I was able to borrow just over $44,000. I used that money to buy another foreclosure with cash. I renovated it and I repeat the process. I have 14 properties now. Twelve of those properties are rentals. I own one small piece of vacant land. I'm not sure what to do with that piece. It came with a purchase of a townhouse. It is too small to build on.

Question 25. How do you manage so many rentals by yourself?

Answer: I find it very easy. The software I use, **Landlord Max**, really increases my productivity and efficiency. I try to automate everything. I also use a lot of templates. I have templates for emails and notices. Every lease violation letter I send looks exactly the same. I just change the name on the template, copy, paste and email. I built a website using the web design tools from the web hosting company. I took the form template and crafted a way for tenants to submit online workorders. Workorders are sent directly to my email account. From there I forward the workorders to a contractor. The contractor contacts the tenant and coordinates repair date and time. I'm completely out of the process. Once the contractor finishes, I pay him using the Cash App by Square. It is all automated and digital. **Speaking of using the Cash App by Square, I collect most of my rent using it.** I invoice tenants from my home office and they pay rent directly into my bank account using the Cash App. I can work in my pjs if I want. I don't but I could. Another thing, my privacy is very important to me. If I'm evicting a tenant for whatever reason, I don't want them coming to my house. For that reason, I rent a PO box from the post office. I use it on my leases and I have all correspondence go to that box. I like it. It helps me maintain my privacy and I find my privacy priceless. I think it is important to regularly inspect my rentals too. I'm in each property, every six months. I do a formal inspection and I change out air conditioning filters. I do not think anyone can expect a tenant to do that stuff. I suppose they can hope but I wouldn't hold my breath. When it comes to the air conditioning systems, I just decided to service them myself during six-month inspections. I change out the air filter and I pour a cup of vinegar down drain lines to kill mildew. I find it helps keep drain lines unplugged. It is a trick I learned from an air conditioning repairman. I notice heating and air conditioning systems result in most of my service calls. I decided it was in my best interest to spend a couple of bucks a year in order to try and keep these systems running. The service calls are really expensive. I also offer complimentary pest treatment during my inspections. I walk around the house and spray indoor pesticide in select places. I spray the kitchens, baths and near entryway doors and patios. I want tenants to have a nice pest free home. I want to help make that happen. I find all of these amenities reduce my vacancy rate. I feel like tenants feel appreciated and valued. I take their patronage seriously. I'm grateful for it because it helps me provide for my own family. We are dependent on each other. We should do right by each other. One other thing before I forget, I drive by the outside of my rentals monthly. I check the grass and try to stay ahead of code enforcement. If code enforcement sees grass that is too long; they sent written citations to me. Citations cause me stress and stress isn't fun. I want to have stress-free rentals. I help keep my stress levels low by enforcing little things on my leases. Enforcing little things keeps small problems from turning into something a lot larger. Lastly, I take a lot of digit pictures to document the condition of the rental. It will help me if I ever have to go to court and try to recover damages. I haven't had to go yet but I will be ready if I do.

Question 26. How do you keep your best tenants?

Answer: I strive to offer an incredible value. I don't think any rentals in the area can stand up to mine. Occasionally, there might be a better-looking property on the market but I will crush the competition with price and overall value. I offer more amenities too. I cannot think of a competitor offering free pest treatment and air conditioning service every six months. Most of the time, these are tenant expenses. **At every lease renewal, I will spend some money on capital improvements.** This keeps tenants happy and it virtually eliminates the need for full remodels. I keep my properties up-to-date and competitive at all times by doing little upgrades annually. During the Christmas season, I will send a postcard. Sometimes I will bake my residents cookies or I will send them a gift card. It is little gestures like these that makes my customers feel appreciated and valued. I truly do value them. I don't go up on the rent every year either. I suppose I could but I'm really in this business for more than just profits. I want to be their #1 housing provider of choice. I really believe we can all improve our quality of life together. If my property taxes or if inflation really jump up; I will pass these expenses over to my tenants. However, if the increases are marginal or negative, I won't raise rent just because. Long-term tenancy is important to me. Quality care and peaceful enjoyment of my rentals are important to me. Maximizing my profits at the expense of people isn't. There are tons of folks who disagree with me on this. That is fine. They can chase profits. I feel I have a social responsibility to my fellow man. It is tough out there. The gap between rich and poor is large and it is growing every day. Maybe I can make a difference, maybe not. The important thing is I will try.

Question 27. How do you handle repairs?

Answer: Carefully. Just kidding, I'm Johnny-on-the-spot when it comes to maintenance. My lease states if something breaks due to fair wear and tear; it is on me. If it breaks due to negligence; it is on the tenant. I have an annual repair and capital improvement budget. **I try to keep the budget around 2.5% of the portfolio's market value.** As the year progresses, I will sometimes spend some of my repair budget on capital improvements and vice versa. Sometimes I bust the budget too. Once I start getting close to popping the budget, I will start to cut costs. Instead of replacing that sliding glass door, I will just repair it. There is always so many things I want to do but so little money to do it. Therefore, I budget and prioritize and I do what I can.

Question 28. How do you handle legal issues like evictions?

Answer: I handle my evictions myself. In Texas, it isn't hard. I send out a 3-day notice by certified mail. After I get delivery receipt, I wait 3 days for their response then I go see the clerk at the Justice of the Peace and file for eviction. A court day is given to me. In the time between filing and the court day, the Constable serves my tenant a summons. We both show up in court and tell our side of the story. I take copies of leases, rules and regulations, emails, text messages, photos and tenant statements as evidence. When it comes to larger legal issues, I hire a competent real estate attorney to represent my interests. When it comes to threating legal action letters or demand letters, I usually handle those things myself. I really try to be intimately familiar with Texas Property Code. It keeps me out of trouble and it keeps me doing everything correctly. I took a lot of time learning about the process of civil litigation before I started my business. I wanted to be familiar with the steps leading from disagreement to the actual courtroom. There are plenty of free sources on the internet outlining the process for anyone interested. I think all real estate investors or real estate professionals should be interested in the process.

Question 29. When it comes to remodels and repairs, how do you keep your expenses down?

Answer: **I standardize everything.** I use the same paint in all my properties. I use the Glidden paint/primer semi-gloss, pure white. It mixed at the factory and it is a perfect white every time. I use a standard white light fixture. I use standard white ceiling fans. Once I found a design that works, I use it in every rental. It saves me from thinking about the remodel. It makes my remodel estimates more accurate. It keeps my cost down since I can buy these standard materials in bulk. When tenants turnover, I already have the paint and it is a perfect match. If a ceramic tile is busted or cracked, I have extra tiles ready to go. I standardize everything. Why do I use the color white? White is a timeless color. It never goes out of style and it appeals to broad markets. Sure, earth tone colors are in but they cost more and it is doubtful they will still be around in 20 years. I know white will. It has been popular for ages. I buy white light fixtures, white ceiling fans. I paint my cabinets white. I can never have too much of the color white. I negotiate discounts with my contractors too. If I spend money in any business more than a couple of times, I will ask for the owner or manager and I will start negotiating. I will pass them my business card and explain what I do for a living. Right after that, I get down to business and I will ask for any property manager discounts. If they don't have any, I encourage them to start. The majority of the time, this works and I start getting products and services at a discount. Most businesses get it. The best sales are business to business sales.

Question 30. I'm sure you've dealt with some disaster properties? How do you get rid of severe pet odors and things like that?

Answer: I feel like everything can be fixed. Even something as stinky as strong pet odors. I once had a tenant move out and rental stunk really bad like unwashed dog. The first thing I did was I swept up all the dog hair and vacuumed the carpet throughout the property. After that, I applied a heavy dose of Arm and Hammer carpet deodorizer on all carpeted areas. The direction on the box said to vacuum the powder up in a few minutes but I let it sit a few days. Afterwards I vacuumed it up and had the carpets professionally cleaned. I had the cleaners go over the carpet with a half and half solution of vinegar and water. Afterwards, there was a strong vinegar smell throughout the house but once it dried, the odors were gone. Now, I'm considering making the vinegar-water treatment standard procedure to treat all my properties this way after a turnover. The carpets looked so clean and smelled so fresh afterwards.

Question 31. Have you ever purchased a home with foundation problems? If so, how did that work out?

Answer: I have purchased a property with foundation problems. The property was sunk in the ground about four inches. It was a foreclosure and I brought it for about 50% below market value. In the end, I sunk about $30,000 into that property during the renovation. I learned a lot from that project. My foundation estimate was way off. I budgeted $5,000 but it cost me $10,000. I had to install 24 concrete piers all around the house. I chose the concrete piers vs the steel piers due to costs. Steel piers would've cost me $20,000. I have owned that property a couple of years now and I still haven't realized a profit on it. With the house moving like it was, it caused a water supply line to break under the slab. Fortunately, I had a good plumber. He abandoned the old supply line and installed a new one so I didn't have to break through the slab to plug the leak. The property still moves some each year. I understand from professionals in the industry, it is hard to fully stop a house from moving. I was told I need to go all the way to bedrock to do it. I was told the bedrock is about 30 feet down or so at that house. I don't have any plans to go that deep right now. I monitor the settlement and I have a structural engineer walk through it every three years or so. It is part of the warranty from my original foundation repair. After this experience, I'm more cautious about purchasing property with foundation issues. I feel like I will do it again but I need to get it at a good price in order to reduce my risk. I probably should've gotten my property with foundation issues about $5,000 cheaper.

Question 32. When it comes to math and numbers, what do you think are the most important numbers to know, understand and track?

Answer: When it comes to income property, **I think the two most important calculations are return on investment (ROI) and cash on cash (CoC) return hands-down.** I feel like every real estate investor needs to know, understand and be able to compute these figures. I like to get my money back from an investment in five years or less. I like a cash-on-cash return above 20%. That is why I don't buy many properties every year. I think the most I've purchased in a given year is three simply because I can't make the numbers work for most properties. I firmly believe it is much better to have a small, highly profitable portfolio than a large portfolio of real estate that barely breaks even. I think investors with slim profit margins are walking a dangerous line. Any unexpected catalyst could cause their whole house of cards to fall apart.

Question 33. How do you personally calculate market value of real estate?

Answer: **The only way to get an official appraisal is by hiring a state licensed real estate appraiser.** However, I don't purchase formal appraisals myself; I estimate market value instead. I assume risk by doing this but I'm ok with it. I know I can over/under estimate market value without an official appraisal. The risks are I may over pay for property or I could unintentionally sell it below market value and leave money on the table. Like I said, I'm ok with risk. It is my money to gain or lose. For the most part, I feel like I'm good at estimating values anyway.

When I had an active real estate license, I'd estimate values by looking at similar properties that sold in the past. I used MLS data. I pulled properties from the database that sold in the last six months, in the same neighborhood, around the same age, with similar characteristics. That means I would only compare a duplex with a duplex or a house with a house. I'd ensure both properties were in the same neighborhood and built around the same time. I'd make sure the buildings have the same number of bedrooms and are close to each other in square footage. I'd use at least three comparable properties; most of the time, I used more.

Then, I'd employ simple arithmetic. I'd calculate a price-per-square foot value for each property. Out of my comparable properties, **I'd find a median price-per-square foot value and I'd multiply that price per square foot value to the square footage of the property I planned to buy.** It gave me an estimate of market value but it was only an estimate. Like I said, I'm ok with risk.

When I don't have MLS access, I use the same method, except I use current listings off of Zillow posted by real estate agents. I figure real estate agents calculate their list price using current MLS data. So, I'm guessing their list price is pretty close to recently closed real estate sales. **Honestly, I'm just guessing market value based on data.** I do the best I can. It has worked for me so far.

This concludes my Q&A session. If I get more questions, I may update this part in future editions. If readers want to submit questions for consideration, please email to kevin.mcneely@kevinmcneelyproperties.com.

Conclusion

Real estate isn't private jets and mansions. It isn't always glamourous. I've never let late night infomercials fool me. Its not a passive activity either. I have learnt this over time. Rather than think about what it isn't, I like to think about what it is.

Real estate is a valuable commodity but it is much more than that. It is someone's home, it is where their life happens. I consider it a great honor to be entrusted with real estate and I care for accordingly.

In the true spirit of business, everyone wins. This has been one of my life's greatest lessons. Great deals equate to great rentals. Great rentals equate to great homes for those in need. In the true spirit of business, customers matter. People are more than a series of numbers, divided into columns on a financial statement. They are more than profit and loss. People, and their quality of life matters. The strange thing is if you focus on doing good and making a difference; profits come without much effort. It is a peculiar side effect of good business and it is an interesting fact of life.

As income inequality rises, property owners have greater impact on what our country becomes. They can use their property and land rights for good by providing quality housing for others or they can use it negatively by milking our population and its people for profits.

I know everyone leaves this earth with a zero-bank account balance. I know it is impossible to take wealth with me. Therefore, it is important I use my resources to make a difference. It is important it mattered that I was here.